The Visit

Donald UpChurch

Copyright © 2013 Donald UpChurch.

All rights reserved. No part of this book may be reproduced, stored, or transmitted by any means—whether auditory, graphic, mechanical, or electronic—without written permission of both publisher and author, except in the case of brief excerpts used in critical articles and reviews. Unauthorized reproduction of any part of this work is illegal and is punishable by law.

ISBN: 978-1-4834-0081-5 (sc)
ISBN: 978-1-4834-0080-8 (e)

Library of Congress Control Number: 2013912369

Because of the dynamic nature of the Internet, any web addresses or links contained in this book may have changed since publication and may no longer be valid. The views expressed in this work are solely those of the author and do not necessarily reflect the views of the publisher, and the publisher hereby disclaims any responsibility for them.

Any people depicted in stock imagery provided by Thinkstock are models, and such images are being used for illustrative purposes only. Certain stock imagery © Thinkstock.

Lulu Publishing Services rev. date: 8/9/2013

Dedication

I would like to thank and dedicate this book to my late wife, Debbie, for giving me the strength and courage to follow my dream of writing. She was a fine artist in her own right. She is missed dearly each day. Debbie fought a fierce battle with breast cancer. She pioneered through the world of alternative medicine. She dared to step out of the norm and ventured around the world bringing doctors together who all have a common goal, defeating cancer. She was the most beautiful woman I have ever known. Those who got a chance to meet her were touched by her generosity and love.

I would also like to dedicate this book also to my mom, Betsy Blake. She always told me I was special and that I could do anything if I put my mind to it. She taught me to follow my dream no matter how long it takes.

Another special dedication goes to my two wonderful children, Heather (Nicki) Nicole and Chazz Christian UpChurch. I have always believed that everyone has a destiny whether it is big or small. They grew up with me telling them they had 'Special Minds' and with that special mind they could create or be whatever they chose in this life. Their destiny is in their hearts and souls to develop and share with this world.

Author's Special Notes

I hope you like this short, but inspirational story. It is my gift to you in hopes that you can find yourself somewhere in this story as well. I have written this story from my heart. It is not meant to push any one religion but it is written out of love to show that we are all connected.

I am donating all of the net proceeds from the sale of 'The Visit" to a foundation that my late wife wanted so desperately to start. It will be called the 'The Deborah Lynn Magoon Alternative Medicine for Cancer Foundation'. Her dream was that everyone should be able to afford any type of treatment that has been proven effective in the dealing with cancer. There are so many people who cannot not even afford regular treatment or their insurance is tapped out. This Foundation will bring hope and hopefully save lives by supplying or supplementing the necessary funding for those beautiful souls.

If you like this book, please encourage your friends to get it as well, so that we can all make a difference one book at a time.

Thank You
Donald

I

"Darn it!" I screamed as I stumbled across the bedroom floor after almost tearing off my little toe on the desk's front leg. *What a way to start the day!* I thought. I sat on the edge of the bed and looked at my pounding toe.

Shoot, I probably broke it. I reached over and touched it. "Ouch!"

I sat for a few minutes until I got used to the pain. I finally got dressed, grabbed my keys, and headed out the door. My foot was aching, and each step was a reminder of how my day was beginning. I got in my car and headed to work. I would be interviewing job applicants most of the morning. I really did not give a rat's butt about it.

My day was starting off the same way my life had been going the last few months. Nothing was going right. Everything seemed to be out of sync. It had been six months since my wife, Debbie, had passed away from cancer. My emotions were all over the place. I tried to cope, but her death and the financial strains of my new business were weighing me down like a chain around my neck in a pool of water. Sometimes I felt like I couldn't breathe, like I was drowning. My memory was slipping too. And my mood swings had my family wondering if I was going to get through it. Hell, to tell the truth, sometimes I wasn't sure I would make it.

They tell me grief is a process I must go through, but I could not buy that anymore. I couldn't put my finger on it. I was not sure if it was depression, grief, stress, or all of the above—but something had to give. Maybe I was telling myself I needed a change. I want to say that I was looking for answers, but hell, I still hadn't figured out the *questions* yet. Even though nothing made any sense and it was hard to put my finger on the problem or problems, it was very hard to describe my life or my feelings at that time. I felt like I had been in a rut. Something was missing, a lacking of sorts . . .

Okay, enough of the daydreaming crap. I had to get on with the day. As the old saying goes, "Same sh—, different day."

Yes, that was the way I thought. My mind never stopped. It seemed like I was always wondering, always thinking. I wanted to be this great, lovable, spiritual-minded person, but then I did things that blew even my own mind. Sometimes I felt it was impossible to live the good life. It was as if I had a daily battle going on inside of me.

I know—great spiritual person, right? Maybe it was just me going through the grief. I didn't know anymore. I mean, I was even mad at God. How would God ever want someone like me? There had to be a God, right? I was brought up in a Southern Methodist family. I went to church on Sundays. I prayed with Debbie every day for God to heal her. I still prayed every day after her death for God to help me get through this mind-overload experience. I wanted to have faith, but my lack of faith made me question everything—even God's existence. But nevertheless, without fail, every day I seemed to talk to him and Jesus. I carried on these conversations with them. Sometimes, I felt like I was that homeless guy walking down the street talking to himself. I must have looked like that at times. I even talked to myself when I was in my car. Thank

God for Bluetooth now. I had so many questions. Hell, why would God talk to *me*, anyhow?

Okay, I did feel a little guilty when I thought and talked in this way. The strange thing was that every time I asked for help, something or someone came along and I was saved for the moment. Well, maybe that was my answer. But it was still not enough for me. I had questions, and I wanted answers.

I was always brought up to believe in Jesus. When I was around four years old, my mom told me that my imaginary friend was Jesus. She said I would talk to him as though he were right there in the room with me. Maybe he was. Go figure! Fifty years later, and I was still talking to him. For every question I have had in life—or just to blow off steam—I have directed my talks to him. He never answers me, but I talk to him. And now I have found myself talking with Debbie too. Maybe I *was* no different from that homeless man talking to himself. I asked Jesus to show me a sign or talk to me. Was I praying to just air? I know you have probably been thinking, *This guy needs help!* The fact was—yes, I did. I wanted some godly sign like a big, burning bush, an angel glowing in my bedroom, or God himself talking to me with a voice that would shake the roof. Some faithful, spiritual outlook, I know, but I had a lot of questions that needed answers. There were a lot of *what-ifs*.

Oh, well. Welcome to my mind. Welcome to my world.

I snapped out of my daydream again and looked at my watch. *Damn, I'm late.*

I got into my car and headed toward my office. The day was no different from any other day. The sun was out and the traffic was light. I lived about fifteen minutes from my office. I had my lead foot putting the pedal to the metal, along with that pounding broken toe. I cruised along and made it to the office with a few minutes to spare.

I grabbed my paperwork, slammed the car door, and rushed in. I said my hellos to the others in the front office and then proceeded to my office where I shut the door and went over to my desk. I sat down, rubbing my eyes while I waited for my computer to come on. I leaned over with my hands on my forehead. I took my shoe off to give my toe a breather. It was still throbbing with this annoying pain. It was not going to let me forget it. I was sitting down, just trying to get ready for the day. *Lord, just get me through today.* There I went again, talking to him as if he had nothing better to do than watch me each morning.

Then there was a knock on my door. I was thinking I

was not ready for the day. I started to say, "Come in," but when I looked up, a man I had never seen was sticking his head around the crack of the door. *How did he get past my office manager?* I wondered. He opened the door wider to give himself room to enter. I set my eyes on him and said sternly but nicely, "Can I help you?"

He passed through the doorway as a smile ran across his face. He was in his mid-thirties to early forties. He looked like he was of Middle Eastern descent, with sharp features and black hair, but the most striking thing was his eyes. They were so blue. Not brown. They seemed to sparkle. His smile was also intriguing; it was a genuine smile that practically lit up his face. There was an energy in it that seemed to soothe me. *Weird!* His appearance was nothing out of the ordinary. He dressed like any other applicant. In fact, he was dressed down for the occasion. He wore blue jeans and a blue collared shirt with white stripes.

He walked up to speak. "It is good to see a man taking care of business!" he replied, still smiling as he entered my office.

I didn't have time for small talk and, frankly, I was not in the mood to talk to anyone, not even the interviewees waiting for me. I looked back at him and asked, "Do you have an appointment for an interview?"

Again his eyes and smile interrupted my thoughts. *What was with that?* I caught myself being drawn in as if he were hypnotizing me.

"No, but I did come to see you, Donald. I am so glad to we can finally meet face to-face." He reached out to shake my hand.

He didn't look at all like a salesman.

"Do I know you?" I asked.

"Well, sort of. We have talked in the past."

The answer was odd. I had never met this man before in my life. This was all I needed right off the bat—some guy wandering into my office unannounced like this. My state of mind was already on the brink of explosion. *Just wait 'til I get in front of my office manager,* I thought.

"And your name?" I asked, feeling more agitated about being bothered by someone who had just snuck into my office. "I am sorry, but you must be mistaken. I have never met you before, and we have never spoken to each other in the past. I'll tell you what—I need you to leave now."

His hand was outstretched, still waiting for my handshake.

I stood up to lead him out of my office. I came around from my desk, trying not to get all caught up in his eyes and smile. When I got in front of him, he grabbed my hand. He held it with both of his hands.

"My name is Josh," he said, smiling and looking as if he were shaking hands with a celebrity. "It is so good to finally meet you. And yes, if you can give me a moment, you will see we do have a lot to talk about." I slowly took my hand away from his. His hand had felt soft but strong. At that moment I didn't feel intimidated by him.

"Are you sure you have the right Donald, Josh? I don't even know you."

He motioned for me to sit down. Can you believe the nerve of this man? I couldn't believe he just motioned me to sit down in my own office. I just wanted to get this man out of my office as quickly as I could.

"Josh, I have a room full of people to interview. I don't want to be rude, but I do not have time for all of this. Please go outside and make an appointment with my office manager. Then we can talk." I pointed to the door, gesturing for him to leave. "Please leave."

I turned and went back to my chair and sat down. I looked up, hoping he had gotten the hint—but no, he was *still there*. My God, how much more direct did I have to be with this guy? He then came in front of my desk and stood over me with both hands on my desk.

"Donald, I do not have a lot of time, either. I am here because you asked me to come."

"I *what?* Asked you to come?" I answered, shaking my head in disbelief.

"Donald, I know this is going to sound a little strange at first, but I need you to listen to me for a minute. If you don't like what you hear, then I will leave and promise not to bother you anymore. Is that fair enough? *Five minutes*, and if you do not want to hear anymore, I will leave." He raised his eyebrow, looking for an approval from me.

Well, I had to give this guy credit for being so persistent. I considered his request. Oh hell, *why not?*

"Okay, five minutes, Josh—five minutes!" I leaned back in my chair after conceding to his offer.

"Great! Donald, like I said before, this may sound a little strange, but it is true. Here goes. I was sent by God to speak to you." He smiled with much enthusiasm.

Oh no, I thought. *He is one of those religious goofs, man. I should have known it.* I snapped back, "I think you are probably sincere and a nice guy"—though *weird* was more the terminology I was referring to under my breath—"but I don't have time to be saved today, and right now I am not in the mood to talk about any religion. I'm sorry, but I really don't have t—" He cut me off instantly.

"Please, hear me out!" he said. "Wait. Over the years, have you been asking some pretty heavy questions? You *have*, haven't you?"

"Well, yes, but who hasn't?"

"True, but you have been uneasy about something for months now. You are not sure what it is, but something is uneasy within your soul right now, right?"

I sat back down, thinking about what he had just said. I nodded.

"Even a good psychic could come up with that." I smirked.

"Don't you believe your prayers could have been heard and just maybe, well, they are now being *answered*, Donald? That maybe God has granted your wish? You wanted to hear directly from him," he continued, stretching his arms out as he looked down at himself, "and he has given you your wish."

"Wait a minute!" I exclaimed. "You are trying to tell me that *God* sent you to give me answers and to tell me things? Why? I am not even a good Christian. In fact, I suck at living that way of life. In fact, my whole life sucks right now."

"Well, God knows that you are struggling. We all think you are ready to listen to him. I am here to offer more truth and knowledge to give you better insight into God's plan for you." Josh meant what he was telling me. He was excited for me. He leaned closer to me and said, "So God is granting your wish. You said to yourself that you could not tell if the messages were coming from your mind or from God? That right?" His eyes were now locked right on mine.

I just sat there, stunned. *Wait a minute. What did I just hear this man say? Did I just hear him say he was sent here by God himself to talk to me?* I didn't know whether to run for the door, scream for help, or believe him. *This is crazy*, I thought, and yet I felt comfortable with him. Then he broke the silence that had felt like an eternity.

"Donald, are you not going through a hard time with your feelings being jumbled all over the place? You grieve over the loss of your wife and you cannot keep your mind from racing at night," he said in an almost accusatory tone, pointing his finger at me as if I were a suspect under interrogation.

"You have been attending two churches with totally different doctrines and you are not even sure which one is right for you. You are even questioning God's existence. You are even questioning your belief in Jesus too—right?

Your beliefs are right in the middle of both of those religious doctrines and you have prayed for help, right, Donald?" he asked, raising an eyebrow. "Am I right, Donald? Just tell me—yes or no?" Just as a lawyer does, he rested his case.

"W-w-well, y-yes," I stammered. "But how could you have known this?" I shouted. "Who really sent you here? Is this some kind of sick joke?"

I was now very defensive and tired of hearing all of my troubles thrown in my face by a complete stranger. I stood up ready to defend myself and to escort this man out of my office. I had heard all I wanted to hear. I came over and reached for his arm to grab him and send him on his way. As I approached him, he just stood there steadily. There was no fight or emotion in his posture, and his eyes were filled with compassion. He was still standing, waiting for that answer from me. I got in front of him and went to grab his arm, but he placed his hand on my shoulder, and a surge of energy or *something* immediately went through my entire body like an electric shockwave, making me calm. My body just completely relaxed, and all the mixed emotions of fear and anger dissipated. My eyes were fixed on him in shock as he kept his hand on my shoulder. He then slowly stood back after I had calmed down and regained my composure. It felt like a surge of calm had come over me—like I had been drugged. I had never felt anything like that before. *Who is this guy?* I wondered.

"Donald, listen. I am here because you repeatedly asked for God to talk to you. He sent me instead. I will leave if you wish, but I would rather stay and complete our conversation. I have much to tell you. But I have only a little time so I will let you choose. What will it be?"

I stood there looking as if I were in a dream. Did I want this man to leave? My face must have looked twisted. It felt like my jaw was at my chest. This could not really be happening to me, but it was, right here in my office. It was something I had asked for all my life. But the rational side of my brain was saying, *This is crazy, insane!* My heart side was telling me to listen to what this stranger had to say. *If it were really true, what insights would I receive? If he isn't telling the truth, what do I have to lose?* I was weighing it out between my rational and emotional selves. Wow, an actual conversation with God or Jesus where there was an actual dialogue between the two of us. I never really thought it could happen, though. My rational side kicked in. *No, this is not real! I cannot believe I am actually falling for this! I cannot believe this is happening to me. Especially now, fifty-five years into my life!*

I walked back to my desk, sat down, and rubbed my forehead with my hands. I tried to reconcile the rational part of my brain with the sentimental part of my heart. I looked back up at Josh as he patiently waited for me to answer him. I studied him for a second. He was no threat. Then, like a child beginning to confess the truth, I let my sentimental side win.

"Okay, yes, I want to know more," I relented, looking at him with a pleading look. "This isn't a joke, is it?"

As I looked up, he was smiling at me. He started laughing quietly at first and then bursting loudly.

"Good choice, my son, and *no, this isn't a joke.* I assure you I am real! This is all happening to you. It is your gift from God. I was hoping this would be your answer. I think you are now ready. I have come to set you on a wonderful journey."

This is so crazy, I thought. However, my gut was telling me I had just made a good choice. Call it a hunch. I even felt a little calmer inside as well.

Who is this guy? I wondered. I looked over at him. He just stood there and smiled a comfortable smile.

"Listen, I still have these interviews to do before I can talk with you, okay?" I reminded him.

He nodded. "How about lunch then?"

"That sounds great," I answered, smiling at him as we headed for my office door.

"I do not want to stop a man from getting his duties done. I will be outside of your office at lunchtime. Then we will talk." He grabbed my hand once again, shaking it with both of his.

"Oh-h-h, Donald, this has made me so happy!"

He let go of my hand. He gave me a thumbs-up and headed out the door, leaving the office. He said good-bye to everyone in the office, shaking hands before leaving—like a politician running for office. Everyone turned to me as I stood there motionless in the doorway. I shrugged, as if I weren't sure who—or *what*—had just left. I turned to go back to my desk and sat down.

What had just happened seemed to be something out of a script of *The Twilight Zone*. A man comes into my office and tells me he was sent by God to give me some answers to my lifelong questions. He touches me. Something happens to me. I become calm. I then tell this man I will meet him for lunch later to carry on the conversation. *Am I crazy?* I wondered. *Is this for real?* I looked around and realized it *was* real. I noticed also that I felt better than I had at the start of my day. *Wait just a minute,* I thought. I wiggled my toe. It didn't hurt at all. *That is strange, very strange indeed—but also very interesting. I think I'll remember this day for a long time.* I smiled to myself and got ready for the first interview.

II

The next few hours, I was busy taking care of business. I went through each interview. I caught myself drifting back at times to my earlier visit with Josh. The morning had been a blur. However, I met each applicant with a smile and found myself in a much better frame of mind. I had just finished an interview when my office manager knocked on my door to tell me I had just one more person to interview. I had coded the interviewee's applications according to my preference and handed them over to her. I asked her to send in the last applicant. In fifteen minutes

I was through with the last interviewee and was done with what I had been dreading all morning. In fact, I had actually *enjoyed* the interviews. I listened to these people. It's not that I didn't enjoy meeting people or interviewing, but it was the thought that it would be *me* who decided who got the job that I didn't like. Everyone I met really needed that job. Times were tough and I had only one job available. Hiring and firing were my least favorite things in my job description.

I looked at my iPhone to check the time. It was 11:45 a.m. All morning long I had felt mixed emotions about this man, Josh—this man who said he had been sent by God to help me. I started to second-guess my meeting with him. I think I was a little scared to meet with him—or at least apprehensive. I started to imagine scenarios about our lunch meeting. *I mean, he could be a lunatic just waiting to get me out somewhere in some remote place,* I thought. *Nah, I didn't get that kind of feeling from him. There was something about him—his eyes, his smile. His overwhelming demeanor was that of a real spiritual man. Yeah, like a holy man,* I mused. I opened my office door and headed to the front lobby. I went over and peaked into Glorina's office. I told her I was meeting someone for lunch and would be back later. I headed for the front door and walked outside. The sky was a radiant blue with the sun at its highest point. I looked around and saw no one. I stood there for a moment or two. Josh was nowhere around.

He is not showing up, I thought. *This guy was a fake. I should have known it.* I laughed at myself for believing something so crazy. I reached in my pocket and grabbed my keys. In a way, though, I was actually disappointed that he hadn't shown up. *Man, do I feel foolish or what? I guess it was simply too good to be true. God doesn't send angels or himself anymore to meet and talk to people*, I mused. I headed for the car.

I got into the car and was about to start it up when I heard a tap on the passenger's window. I turned to see blue eyes and a smile gazing down at me. Josh was pointing down at the lock on the door for me to unlock it. I was actually scared at this moment. My legs began to shake as my heart began racing. All kinds of thoughts were going through my head, but the biggest one was: *Is this man an angel of God or what? Had God really sent him down to talk to me, who is of little faith? And if so, why me?*

I opened the car door. He got into the car. I started the car up.

"Beautiful day—isn't it, Donald? His eyes were fixed on the landscape outside the window.

"Yes, it is," I replied. Do you have a preference for lunch?"

"Could we just grab a bite to go? Then maybe go somewhere outside to eat and talk? It would be a shame to waste this beautiful day to sit inside—you agree?"

I nodded my head, thinking of this little diner down the road, not far from a park. I cannot remember the last time I had eaten lunch in a park. In fact, I can't remember the last time I had just spent time outdoors. I used to practically *live* outdoors when I was a child. It was hard for my parents to get me to come inside. But time had changed me; it had changed the wonder inside my soul to explore as I had as a young boy. I saw most of nature now through a window of my car. I had not given it much thought until this moment. It is strange how your life changes and you never reflect on it until it's too late. This was my biggest regret with Debbie dying. Life changed before I had time to reflect on things with her. I was left with the many mistakes I had made, and now I had to live with them. I started to feel sad.

Josh looked like he was studying my train of thought. He must have known what I was thinking, because of—you know—being this person from wherever he came.

"Let's enjoy some time outside like the old days. What

do you say?" Josh's eyes widened, as if saying, "Come on and let's do it!"

I glanced over at him and then back through the window. I nodded my head yes and backed the car out of the parking space. He laughed as we drove out of the parking lot. It was as if he were a little child going on a journey for the first time. His laughter was contagious, and soon a smile ran across my face. Memories began flowing from my childhood. He knew what I was thinking. He must have ESP. His laughter was even more profound.

Leaning toward me, Josh said, "Oh, Donald, this is going to be a great day. I can sense it. Can't you?"

I thought about it for a second, and then excitement came over me—something I had not felt in a long time. Then a smile rose across my face. I began nodding to myself and thought, *Oh yes, I do believe this is going to be a day to remember.*

We picked up our lunch at the diner and headed into the park. We got out of the car and starting walking along one of the paths toward a little pond. We found a bench along the small pond. The pond was filled with lots of lily pads; it was a frog's heaven.

"Ah, the fresh air. Nothing like it!" Josh marveled as he leaned his head back and took in a deep breath of fresh air.

He closed his eyes and just sat there in silence for a few seconds. Then he began to pray a blessing for our food. It took me totally by surprise when he started to pray. I was just about to take my first bite of my turkey club grinder. I immediately closed my eyes, placed my grinder in my lap, and joined him in the blessing.

When he finished, he said, "I bless this food in your name, Father. Amen." He opened his eyes, winked at me, and then took a bite of his vegetarian grinder. He took the first bite and closed his eyes.

"Mm-mm. This is so good."

"How's yours?" he asked, looking over at me with his mouth full.

"It's okay, but it doesn't sound as good as yours!" I couldn't help from laughing. He was savoring every single bite as if he had not eaten in a long time.

"What are you doing?" I asked him, referring to his savoring technique.

He looked a little puzzled at first, not knowing what I was asking about. Then he realized and started talking to me with his mouth full. He put up his hand, finished the bite, and then said, "I am honoring each bite as nourishment for my body." He looked at me and smiled. "It also helps slow me down from eating too fast and getting indigestion!" Then he burst out laughing.

"Lighten up, Donald. Enjoy your meal!" I started to laugh. I really didn't know how to take this man. There was definitely something about him. And that laugh of his was so genuine. It was like listening to a child laughing uncontrollably. It made me feel comfortable.

As we ate, I couldn't help but wonder what this man wanted from me. When would he start? What was he going to say to me? I finished my grinder well before he finished his, since he was savoring each and every bite. Finally, he finished, wiped his mouth with a napkin, and leaned back to let the sun hit his face.

Letting go a heavy sigh, he started talking to me without moving his head so his face could still soak up the sun. It kind of made his face shine with a radiant, golden glow. Even though it was radiant, it was subtle. (Okay, it could have been my imagination too.) He started talking.

"Donald, do you believe in a God as your father of all things?"

"Yes, of course I do! That was what I was taught." I suddenly felt uneasy with the question.

He opened his eyes, lowered his head, and turned to me.

"Why, then, do you not trust him and place your faith in him every day?" he asked, looking intently into my eyes. The question was direct and to the point. I guess he meant to open up the lines of communication between us.

"Well," I answered, looking directly at him, "this is one of the questions I have always asked God or Jesus. Why can't I just trust in God and have faith in him and live the good old *Christian way of life*? Whether I am talking to them out loud or in prayer, I still never get an answer. You see, I have realized I keep trying to control things, situations in my life, my business. I even try to control my own faith. I am a *control freak*. What can I say?"

I glanced over to him. He was still watching my every expression and listening intently to every word coming out of my mouth.

"I guess I have always thought I would be weak to—you know—*let go, let God*. In a way, though, looking back over the years, it has been the pillar for all my downfalls. Funny thing is, I knew it then but still did it, and I know it now and I *still* do it. Sounds strange, huh?"

I looked over at him to see him smiling.

"Not strange at all, but there *is* a question I have for you before we begin today. It is the biggest question I will ask of you. I will need an answer before we start."

I lowered my head, thinking, *Here we go. I knew there was something attached to this!* I looked back up to him and nodded.

He proceeded, "Are you willing to trust and put your faith in him today?"

I turned away quickly for a second, looking out toward the pond and then over to the flowers in the park. My gaze finally came back to Josh, who was smiling as he searched my eyes, waiting for my answer.

My answer was yes, but for some reason I couldn't even say it. I just started nodding my head yes. I am not sure why, but tears welled up in my eyes. I felt this overwhelming sense of release surging all over my body. A surge of emotions seemed to float to the top. I felt this sense of wanting to let everything inside of me go. The more I thought about it, the more emotional I became. It is hard to describe—but it felt like pure joy, not sadness. I then started to cry uncontrollably—like a blubbering idiot, in fact. *Stop this*, I thought, trying desperately to wipe the tears from my face. I had not done this since I was a child. Man, this was embarrassing.

"Wow!" I exclaimed, wiping my tears away. "I can't believe I'm doing this." I leaned my head back.

"Whew! I guess that answers my first question, huh?" I said, regaining my composure.

Josh put his arm around me and said, "No—that, my son, is *letting go and letting God*."

III

It did not take long to realize that Josh was no ordinary man. He was indeed a special man. Maybe he was an angel or some kind of spiritual, holy man here on earth to channel messages from God. Whoever he was, I knew he meant me no harm. He just sat there patting me on the back, letting me regain my composure; there was no judgment. Surprisingly, my embarrassment vanished, leaving me instead with a sigh of relief. We just sat there for those few moments in silence.

"You know," I said, looking out toward the pond after pulling myself together, "I have asked God all my life to just show me. Just *show* me if I am doing the right thing. What am I on this earth to do? What's my destiny? Why do I do the things I know are wrong? Then, when I act on the thing I am praying about, I begin to wonder if I am controlling that situation or if it is the divine plan that God has for me. I never get a true answer." I looked directly at him. "Why?" I asked, feeling myself getting edgy. Josh kept smiling, leaning back, and facing the sun, letting it hit his face. I continued.

"It says in the Bible that if you ask, you will receive, doesn't it? I haven't received any answers. Because of that, I have failed more than I have succeeded, and—believe me—I have asked for his guidance more than once. Why would he let me go through all these failures?"

"Okay, hmm, let me see if I can say this to you in a way you will understand," Josh said, still closing his eyes and leaning back to get more sun. He turned toward me and began to speak.

"Donald, the right thing to do for yourself is to live and learn. Sometimes you need to look at your life as a movie picture on a big screen, sit back, and just let your mind flow through all those memories. You see, there are patterns in your life. There are patterns for the times you succeed and patterns when you fail. There are patterns when you love someone, and there are patterns when you get hurt. These patterns were developed while you were living and learning. And through all this process you also are trying to find your relationship with God—and then, well, another pattern starts. When you start to notice the patterns that are not good for you, you must learn to change them. This is easier said than done, but it is necessary for you to have any growth spiritually. Donald, the path to live within God's holiness is very narrow, but the rewards are more than one can comprehend. Your patterns that you develop along the way in life are often too broad to follow God's path of righteousness. That is why you keep doing things you know you should not do. Sometimes you are so distanced from God, you never hear his messages. But all in all, he patiently waits."

He shifted a bit to get the sun out of his eyes and then continued.

"You see, this is all because he has given you free will. He loves you and wants you to love him, but nonetheless, he gives you free will to choose. Then—as far as the question of *what is your destiny?* I will say this: all people have a God-given talent inside of them. That talent is the key to their destiny. Some find their talent early in life, others find it later, and then some *never* find it, I am sad to say. In order to discover it, one must truly believe in God and in oneself. It is a dynamic duo. God also knows what prayers need to be answered. Take yourself—you said that you have failed more than you have succeeded, right?"

I nodded my head yes, but I was still trying to absorb what he had just said.

He continued, "Without failure there could be no success! Now let me say that again—*without failure there could be no success*. Your failures are God's stepping-stones; they are for those who brush themselves off and keep going. Let me ask you something, Donald. Have you learned from your past failures?"

I thought for a second and said, "I think I've learned from most of them. The ones I didn't learn from seem to show up in other ways in my life."

"Precisely!" he said, pointing his index finger at me. "Then just maybe your answers were in your *failures* as well successes."

He grinned, knowing that he had just stimulated my intellect. I looked over at him and smiled. He knew I was getting what he was saying.

"I hope this has helped you with your question, but to tell the truth, there are far more important things that

God wants from his children. He wants you to learn to love unconditionally—both him and your neighbor—as yourself. He wants you to love yourself. He wants you to be happy."

"Wow, I guess maybe my question was selfish then, huh?" I remarked, feeling a little regret.

"Absolutely not, Donald. It was the right question to ask. No question is wrong, because there are so many others asking the same thing as you. I have answered you but have left the work that needs to be done up to you.

"You see, I can give you divine truths all day, but at the end of the day, it is *you* who will choose to believe to follow the truth or not. Remember? Free will?" He continued, "My mission today is to help you to open your eyes to the knowledge and truth that is out there to be received. Donald, the truth is not hidden out there somewhere buried in some cave in the desert or written on some church in Scotland. The truth is in plain sight for those who seek it with all their heart and soul."

Now he leaned back into the sun. With his eyes closed again, he added, "Always has been and always will be. It is his promise to you."

He then smiled, got up off the bench, and started to

stretch. He shook his legs about and bent over to touch his toes. I just sat there trying to absorb the information he had just given me.

At that moment, I noticed an old man coming along the path. He was wearing an old fishing hat, and his white hair hung over his ears. His back was bent with years upon him. You could tell he was struggling a bit. He still managed a smile, though. He stopped at the pond and fed the ducks. He reached over and smelled a flower that was growing right at the water's edge. You could tell he was enjoying his surroundings.

He looked over at us and waved. "Beautiful day!" he said, beaming. "The Lord has given me this day to enjoy, and that's just what I am here to do." He had a big smile on his face as he walked toward us. We greeted him with a smile, and Josh observed, "It looks like you are a man full of gratefulness."

"Amen to that," the old man answered. "The Lord keeps me here until he's ready for me to come home to him." He grinned at me and added, "I am ready when he is, that's for sure." He turned to look at the pond and then looked over at the flowers that were blooming.

"I will miss all this about a fraction of a second when I *do* go, because God's home is a thousand times more beautiful," he said thoughtfully.

I could tell he was a man who would tell you what he thought—whether or not you wanted to hear it. I smiled at the thought.

Josh went over to him. "You have served our father well, Gerald. He loves you, you know that?"

The old man nodded. The strange thing is, I never heard him mention his name to us. *How did Josh know it?*

"Hey, my friend here," Josh said, pointing over to me, "is starting to question just what God wants from him. You have been around a long time. Do you have any suggestions for him?"

"Yes, I sure do—and it's simple,"

Gerald pointed his index finger at me as he spoke.

"Put the Lord first in your life—*that's* what you do, young man. Love everyone and forgive anyone! It's that simple."

He choked up and said, "He loves you, boy. He loves you! Never forget that, and nothing will ever take you down. Remember, it takes some of us a lifetime to learn the lessons that God has for us. You just have to be a willing student and love him. Then you will receive his blessings."

I just sat there taking in what this old gentleman had just

told me. I couldn't help but admire his convictions. He was so sincere. I felt humbled at that moment—being with two people who had so much dedication to God.

"Thank you, sir. Thank you for the advice."

"Well, I mean it," he snapped back quickly, regaining his composure. "I have to be on my way. See you fellas around. It's been nice talking with you."

Josh responded with a wave. "God bless you, Gerald!"

He turned around and waved back at us. Then he was gone.

Josh turned backed to me.

"Now, where do we go from here?" Josh asked.

I thought for a few moments and then remembered something the old man had just said: "Love everyone and forgive anyone". *Was that old man an angel too? Was he sent to give me the next question I needed to ask?*

Yeah, right, I thought to myself sarcastically. *Forgiveness—that's a good one.*

"I guess my next question would be about forgiveness," I told Josh.

"Good subject," he said, nodding his head. "What is the question you have for me?"

"I want to know why it is so important to forgive others

who have done me wrong. I mean, *family* I can see forgiving, but what about when someone made it a point to hurt or harm me? How am I supposed to forgive them? Please don't give me the answer that it says to do so in the Bible, either. I already know that. What is the universal reason to forgive?"

I noticed how worked up I felt inside just thinking about forgiveness. This question had my emotions flying about inside of me like a sparkler on the Fourth of July. I have had close friends—even family members—just step all over my heart and soul. It has left me with many bitter memories. It left me angry. I prayed through the years about this subject. Forgiveness does not come easy for me. It never has.

Josh could sense my edginess. "Well, okay then. Look at yourself right now. How do you feel right this moment?"

"I'm angry. And I'm hurt, damn it . . . Oh, sorry about saying that, but it brings up memories of when others have done me wrong. It makes me pissed. What can I say? It makes me tense, and then I get worked up."

I looked away and stared into space. I really could feel this building up inside of me. Usually, I am somewhat of an easygoing guy, but there are times when I do get myself worked up. This was one of them.

"Donald, is it worth losing sleep over, even years after it has happened?"

"I don't lose sleep over it," I answered. "I really don't think about it much, but you asked me to ask the question. I guess the bad memories and feelings came back for a moment, but I let them go a long time ago."

"No, you haven't. That is just the point," Josh said gently. "They are still in you. They have left you with these trigger points, and when they get pushed, the memories—along with all their emotions—come back to haunt you. It's baggage!"

He was now pressing me to look at him. I knew he was right, although I did not want to admit it. The tone of his voice was compassionate. He knew I was hurt. I was mad. This was a harder question than I thought it would be. I looked up at him. His ice-blue eyes were looking at me as if he were feeling my pain.

"Donald, we must learn to forgive in order to move on in our lives spiritually. Forgiveness is more for the person who is doing the forgiving, rather than the one receiving it. Forgiveness keeps the baggage out of your heart and mind. It keeps your emotions in the present and not in the past. Just like *right now*, for instance. You have to let it go and forgive, and then you are almost free!"

I looked at him a bit confused. I understood everything he had just told me. It would be hard at first, but I knew I had to do it. What did he mean by his last statement, though? That was confusing. What did he mean by his statement: "Then you are almost free?" I was sitting there on that bench when he rose up and motioned for me to walk with him through the park. As we started walking, I was about to speak when he interrupted me.

"Donald, the most important thing I want to tell you about forgiveness is about *you*." He continued, "You must forgive *yourself* first. You must forgive yourself of all those skeletons that lie in your closet. You must forgive yourself of the mistakes you made with your wife, Debbie. When I said *almost free*, this is what I meant. Do you want to know how to do it?"

I looked at him. "Pray about it, right?"

"Well, you are on the right track, but the way to really forgive yourself is to tell God about everything you have been ashamed of by sharing your dark past. He already knows what your past is, but by you sharing it with him out loud in prayer, God will turn your darkness into light, so you will never have to bear the guilt or shame again. You must ask him out loud to forgive you for everything. God will forgive you, because he loves you, no matter what you have done in the past—just like a father who loves his children. You love your children, right? When they do something bad, do you stop loving them? Of course not! Unconditional love, remember? Then when you have asked God for his forgiveness, you have forgiven yourself. God will then open up to you all his glory he has for you. Then at last you are free!"

"What about my anger with God?" I asked. "How can I be free of that? I mean, there are things that happen in this world that make me mad at God. I do not understand how all these bad things happen. It is as if God himself is letting them happen. Why would he do that when he can stop anything? And why does he spare this one who has been a menace to the human race but then let the one who serves him *suffer*? I just don't get it!"

I turned my head, feeling that I may have overstepped my boundaries—but the anger flowed through my veins. At least I *thought* it was anger. Maybe it was more hurt than anger.

"Give me a *for instance*," Josh suggested. "I know something is bothering you. What is it really?" I felt Josh's eyes on me until I raised my head and looked back at him. He had an intense gaze on me. It was as if he could feel my pain behind the anger.

"I will never understand how someone who has never really done anything wrong in this world can be struck down with a disease like cancer. I just lost my wife to cancer. She was my soul mate and my life partner. She read all the scriptures of healing and even recorded them; she played them over and over again. She prayed every spare moment for God to heal her like it says in the Bible. She was driven by the word of God. And in the end, she did not get healed. In fact, she died a horrible and painful death right in front of my son, my daughter, and me. She prayed so very hard for God to heal her. She would ask me over and over again to do a healing prayer on her. I felt so helpless. It even says in the Bible that you will be healed if you place your heart and soul to do God's work. Instead I watched her suffer the last year to the point that she drove me away from her. She drove me away!" I was now hollering at him.

"She drove me away! And I did not want that," I cried, through angry tears. "Do you even understand the pain and the hurt I carry around with me now?"

I was right in his face at this point, eye to eye with him. He never lost eye contact with me. He listened intently to all of my outbursts of anger and hurt.

"What is your great divine answer for all the suffering and

pain that we had to see and endure with her at the end of her life?" I asked, unable to hide the scorn in my voice.

"Explain that to me—how God would let that go on. How do I explain to my son now that God is merciful and loving? How do I get him to trust in Jesus again? We just watched her die a sad, horrible death, and you know something? She did not deserve to go that way. I am the one who deserved it more than her. I am the one who drank and took drugs and never took care of my body." Tears from the depths of my soul were running down my face. My grief and emotions burst out like fireworks.

"He took her from us and he could have healed her!" I sobbed, lowering my head into my hands and feeling as if the whole world had let me down.

"This is why I have been questioning his existence. If he is so powerful and loving and all-knowing, why would he do this to his children? To punish me? Maybe. No, God let me down. And now he sends *you* to me to give me more truth and knowledge by answering the questions I have pondered throughout my life? I don't buy it." My burden at this moment was so heavy I felt like I was going to collapse.

I felt Josh's arm come around my back. He started caressing me just enough to let me know he had heard me. I started crying so hard. It was all built up inside of me like a ticking bomb. It was an explosion of emotion and anger. We just continued to sit as I cried. I looked up at one point and noticed that he too was crying right along with me. *Why would he be crying along with me?* I wondered. I hadn't cried like that since I was a young boy. Maybe grief was hitting me between the eyes once again. Uncontrollable pain and sorrow had crept into my heart. And this man—whom I had just met—was crying along with me as if he were feeling every ounce of my sorrow and pain.

He pulled my chin up with his left hand to get me to look in his eyes. He started to say something but took a deep breath instead. He wanted to say something but looked like he was searching for the right words. He then started praying. It was a deep prayer within himself. His lips were moving, but I could not understand what he was praying about. He finally opened his eyes, and they were bluer than ever. The way he gazed at me felt like he was giving me something from his soul to mine. It was weird, but it was as if he gave a piece of himself to me at that moment. I don't know how or what it was, but I could feel his presence within me.

He then took my hands into his and began to talk.

"Donald, first of all, I am sorry for your loss. Death of a loved one is painful, especially when your loved one seemed to suffer until the end. Yes, Debbie was indeed an angel in her own way here."

Josh took a deep breath, letting it out with a sigh. He closed his eyes and then opened them again. "Donald, no words of explanation to this question will take away the pain and grief of losing a loved one. I just want you to know this. Your pain and sorrow that you and your family are going through is real. God feels your loss. He does, however, see things on a grander scale than you can even imagine." He took another deep breath, closed his eyes, and looked deep in thought before proceeding.

"Being healed is not always in the physical realm, because the physical body ages and breaks down over the years. It also comes down with all kinds of disabilities we do not anticipate—along with the diseases that affect it. However, the spirit sometimes has not developed to its full potential. It then becomes trapped, therefore enduring the physical constraints placed upon it. The spirit continues to yearn and seek its development. Do you understand that?" Josh asked, looking over at me. I was still listening, trying to envision what he was saying, but my heart still focused on the anger of her suffering in her last days—and that outweighed his words of wisdom.

"Did God give us the power to heal the physical body or not? Are we not capable of performing miracles ourselves?" I questioned. My voice rising, I continued, "Jesus said, 'These things I do, and you can do even greater!' Was that just a bunch of crap?"

He smiled and nodded that he had heard what I had just said. His face remained calm as he continued to speak. "Donald, this is much more than most can comprehend. I will try to give you the insight so that you might find your own answer within yourself. The answer to your question is yes. God has given us the ability to heal, but the free will of a person can be even stronger than his gift. When you or someone else is faced with a crisis such as a disease like cancer, for instance, it is very tough. The fear creates a lack of faith that gets so deeply seeded within your own mind that you cannot let go of the disease."

I was still trying my best to follow him. I understood that our minds can create our outcomes in life over many things.

"Donald, Debbie could not beat the force of her fear inside of her. Therefore, her faith was blinded by that overwhelming fear. She tried gallantly to battle it, but—like the cancer—it won. I am sorry. God took her because her spirit could no longer be contained inside of the physical body that was so damaged by the cancer. He healed her from the inside so she could now have everlasting life. He loved her as much as you loved her. She never gave up fighting, but instead she transformed. What you saw on the outside was not a battle on the inside. God knows the bigger picture. Someday it will become your time, and then you will know the truth I say to you today."

"You see," he continued, "God created us in his likeness. He placed in each one of us the ability by giving us the most powerful tool on earth. Our brains! The knowledge is there, but unlike God, we do not know how to use its full capacity. Within each of us is the dormant power to conquer all things here on earth. That is, everything except death."

He then turned to me with a sparkle in his eyes—as if he had thought of something great to tell me.

"Do you remember I told you that you needed to sit back at times and look at your life like a movie?"

"Yes."

"Well, let's take a look at the developments we as humans have made over the years. It is right there in front of you if you will just open your inner eye to envision it. Throughout history you can see the development of our use of our brain—and its evolution. Think about this for a minute. The most intelligent men back in the Renaissance period would be blown away by the technology we have developed today. God has given us all the power to connect." He paused before continuing.

"Donald, in the beginning, there was to be no death. We were created in his likeness, and death was not part of the scenario. God gave Adam and Eve the free will to live as they chose—even to eat the fruit from the tree of knowledge—and with it came death and separation from God. I tell you this story because you were raised through your Christian beliefs. There are other stories in other religions as well. They all lead to this.

"You see, God has given each of us free will throughout the history of our existence, and we do ourselves in each and every time we choose to go against God's wishes. So, with that said, I think you see that it is not God's purpose to let terrible things happen. It has to do a lot with the consequences of our free will."

IV

After that heavy and deep conversation, Josh just had us walk. It gave me time to process the feelings I had just been through and to let what he had said sink in. I guess before that day I hadn't looked at the bigger picture of things like Debbie's death. My eyes and soul were indeed enlightened with an understanding that I could comprehend. I guess I was really getting my wish answered today.

We walked down to the path that went along the pond. There were ducks and geese enjoying their little oasis. A mother duck was swimming with her four little baby ducklings. They all stayed very close to her as she swam along the water's edge, keeping her distance from us as we approached. It was a beautiful day. It was in the mid-eighties, with the sun blasting its rays on nature. The only word I could think of to describe this moment was *harmonious*. Birds were singing and seemed to be dancing from tree to tree. A distant croak from a bullfrog on a lily pad seemed to add the bass to a symphony created at that very moment by Mother Nature herself. To our far left were open fields where people played games and had cookouts. I looked up just ahead and saw a little bridge over the pond we had been overlooking while having our lunch. We headed in that direction.

We got to the bridge and walked out onto it. When we reached the middle, Josh stopped and leaned against the rail, looking out toward where we had just been. We stood there for a few moments, taking in nature while I gathered my thoughts about what I had just been told. Even though it had been emotional at times, I really think I was beginning to understand a bigger picture of life other than just mine. I had been so caught up in all the crap that falls in front of you each day. I began to realize that day that all that BS is a trap waiting to snare you into its little tentacles—draining you of the pleasures that are out there right in front of your eyes. *Hmm, interesting,* I thought. I finally spoke up. "I have another question."

"Go ahead," Josh said, acknowledging my request.

I held my breath because this question had stirred up many debates over the years. I admit I wanted to know the absolute truth—you know—the divine truth.

I took a deep breath and said, "There are so many different religions in the world. In Christianity we have the Bible, but it has many different doctrines. There are also many other religions that have their own holy book. They have their own God and their own prophets—the Muslims, Hindus, Jews, Budhists, and the list goes on. They believe theirs to be the only truth as well. Our own Christian Bible has been doctored and altered through the years by both the church and man. We also have had discoveries like the Dead Sea Scrolls, and there are probably many more lost words of God that have long been lost or destroyed through time. I guess my question is this: Is the Bible today—with all of its changes, with gospels left out by the church and man—the word of *God* or the word of *man*? My other question that ties to this question is, What about all the other religions and their doctrines out there in the world? Are they right or wrong? And if they are *wrong*, what will happen to those masses who believe with all their hearts that their God is the only God? And if they are right, where do we stand as Christians—believing that Jesus saved us all from the grips of death and sin? What about Jesus then being the only way to everlasting life? What about the others—Muhammad, Buddha, and so forth? Would it be wrong to assume we have the right religion and the only savior? Through the years I have heard parts of other religions' basic beliefs, and it seems we are all saying basically the same thing when it comes to our universal truth and love."

I had a lot more to ask, but I knew I had given him a series of very tough questions, questions that have sparked wars and death throughout history even up to our present day. I wondered if he would dare tell me the truth—or maybe he didn't know the answers himself.

I studied Josh, who looked as if he were in a deep, meditative state. He stood there motionless for about two or three minutes, leaning on the bridge rail before finally turning around to me. His look was more serious than before. His smile, although weak, was still there. His eyes seemed to be searching me as he began to speak.

"You gave me a lot of very important and serious questions. I can see how the questions kind of fall in line with each other. I want to try to give you the best answer I can give. However,

I want to make this answer so that you will understand the importance of all religions and what they all have for their followers. Okay?"

I nodded, waiting for him to begin. I could see he wanted to be careful with his answer. I wanted to respect that, but I had questions that I had longed to find answers to—questions on religion everyone fights about.

He began to talk.

"First of all, I want to address your question about the Bible—it being doctored, altered, gospels taken out, put in, and so forth. Donald, the Bible is the *word of God*. It still conveys his messages to us throughout the centuries with his children. It can never be altered to the point of taking away his word or the truth. It has always given us an order by which we live as God's children. The lost scrolls and lost words of God throughout the years are indeed accounts of importance as well. God has inspired men throughout time to write on his behalf. Many prophets have been given the duty to speak on God's behalf all around the world. This has developed into many other different cultures and religions. I know by saying this that I will offend many who do not understand the true connection we all have to our father. However, I say this out of love and respect for all. The messages of all that have been written are what God wants us to know and what he inspired to be written. God's anointed ones who brought his messages to their people are very important as well. Each religion does have its own beliefs; some have not heard of Jesus, and many have. As Christians and through your doctrine and beliefs, it leaves a gap from the others. We become puzzled because we have been taught that the only way to God is though Christ Jesus. Many do not understand what his death did for all of God's children including them. The prophets and anointed ones talked about fulfilling the prophecies throughout the world. Jesus came and tied them all together by fulfilling them all, whether they believed it or not. It does not mean that Christianity is the superior religion. Jesus was a *way shower*. He said, 'Follow me!' Jesus himself was a Jew, not a Christian. Are any of God's children condemned for their lack of knowledge? Does God punish them for this? I say no, because it is his love that he gave to each of us when he sent him to die for all of us. He did it unselfishly, lovingly, for all mankind. All religions, their holy books and beliefs, all come to a point. That point is God. He has many names. He had many messengers of truth and love—as Jesus himself and many others spoke of. I say this because we are *all* his children. We were all made in his likeness. We are all brothers and sisters known as the *human race*, not one race better than the other. We all share one thing in common—we inhabit the earth. We are spirits living in human physical form. God loves each and every one of us. He is our father. He shares his love with all of us. We are all connected whether we choose to believe it or not. If a disaster happens halfway around the world, we all feel it; we all share the pain and loss in one way or another. We are all connected to his divine energy."

He then looked back over the pond and stared for a moment or two before continuing. He turned back at me after gathering his thoughts. His smile was much fuller now. His eyes sparkled in the sunlight. He had this look of *knowing*. It was hard to explain, but there was a sureness about him.

He spoke again. "Donald, I know for a fact that Jesus was here. He was sent to help fulfill God's promise to all of his children. He was the son of God. We all are his children. He told the crowds to follow him. He was teaching them how to reconnect with our loving father. He taught and lived among those who were always shunned by the church. He lived basically in the battlefield. Think about it. He never owned a home. He took twelve young men and went around healing and sharing his message: the message of *love*. He was perfect in the image of his father. He knew his destiny and what his mission was, and he did it all the way to the end, to his violent death. His resurrection was giving everyone life and freedom from death and sin, not just one religion. You see, Donald, he did it for all future generations of the entire human race and also for the ones who had died before him. He was the *way shower*. Those of us who get the chance to hear his message are compelled to be baptized by his chosen disciples to give us a new beginning of being renewed. I know this is not what some doctrines believe in. I say that we *all* get baptized when we truly reconnect with the divine energy and love of God. The truth is that *the truth lies within all of us*. For those who believe in their own God, I say we all are his children. God still loves them—their souls will not be cast away—but instead they too have the ability to be shown the truth: the truth that we were all saved by God's love for his children. I am here because I want you to know all of God's children will have a chance to go to heaven. Heaven lies within all of us. We are all his children."

Josh took a long breath and continued. "Jesus's message was to love your neighbor. He talked about it constantly, and it is written throughout the New Testament. Love is also taught in many other holy books around the world. It was taught by Mohammad, Buddha, and many more anointed ones. It is God's message that is written in so many of those doctrines and religions. You must learn to love your neighbor as yourself. *Love* is universal throughout world. In our Bible, in first Corinthians, it says, 'Love does not keep record of wrong.' This is why forgiveness is so important. In the book of Matthew, it says, 'The way you forgive other people is the way God will forgive you.' We lose our way when we do not honor both of these. The lack of these two things creates all the bad emotions such as anger, envy, greed, hurt—and then evil takes control because these emotions keep the light out and the darkness in. But love and forgiveness bring hope and faith, and the darkness cannot survive with all of these in your life. It is the universal truth!"

Josh patted me on the back. I had been in deep thought over all he had just said. I smiled at him. He started to walk past the pond to a path leading up a hill to a garden. The birds were chirping in the trees.

The sunlight was sending beams of light through these trees and shining down to the ground below. They were creating shades of light and darkness. It sort of reminded me of what he had just said.

V

We walked along the path as it winded back and forth up a steep hill leading to a garden. At times it was darker because the trees were denser and less sunlight broke through. It was much cooler in the shade as well. As we broke into the sunlight, it would radiate heat and warm my face. I was still thinking of the message I had just received from Josh.

I felt so much peace at that moment. There was a harmony throughout the park, and I felt I was now a part of it. It was far from the many times I had found myself facing hopelessness and feeling left out. Many times in my life, I had felt as if there were no way out. I felt trapped. The course of my life had led me to that day, to where I was both mentally and spiritually. Some of it was for the good, and a lot of it was for the worse. During some of these times, I felt no faith anywhere around. There were many times when I felt like I had been abandoned by God and left to the wolves. These were the times I was the angriest with him. There were times I had screamed at him for letting me down. I felt a little ashamed of those times as well. Through the years I have repeatedly asked for his forgiveness.

Forgiveness—the word kept popping up. *What had he said earlier?* He had quoted the book of Matthew: *The way you forgive others is the way God will forgive you.*

I turned to Josh, who was now making little birdcall sounds to the birds. I studied him. His eyes were filled with something I had longed for all my life. He had a peace about him. He was a part of the harmony of the surroundings. He was content with just being in the moment, enjoying all of nature and his surroundings.

"Josh, I think my next question is about faith and hope. How can I maintain enough faith to know—to *really* know—that everything will be okay? My faith at many times is nowhere to be found. In the past, I have asked God to please show me a sign or guide me through a particular difficult time. He never gave me an answer. Many times I took hard falls because of not knowing whether or not he was helping me."

He looked at me as if he was questioning what I had just said. I continued, more defensively.

"I am not saying I am blaming God for all my downfalls, but what I *am* saying is that there were times I really needed him. I felt that he was not around. Was it because I had no faith? It left me many times feeling hopeless."

He then nodded that he understood what I was trying to say.

"It felt as if you were a little empty inside, right?" he asked softly, still looking at the birds in the trees.

"It felt like I was alone. God was nowhere around. I mean, he must have been there, but I all I heard was silence." I spoke adamantly, wanting to get my message across.

"What happened to those difficult times you had? Did they turn out as bad as you thought they would?" he probed.

"Well, no, they didn't, but still I felt he had abandoned me somehow," I answered, feeling a bit sheepish about being so adamant with my last statement.

"There were times I really needed something to either

happen or someone to be there for me," I continued. "He didn't seem to hear my prayer at all during those times. There was this particular time when I lost everything. I tried with all my might to save it, but I still lost it all. I lost so much sleep over it. I prayed every single night asking him to just show me what to do, but I never got an answer. I eventually lost everything. What ever happened to 'Ask and it will be given unto you?'"

"He did answer you, Donald. It just wasn't what you wanted to hear or have happen." In a now matter-of-fact tone, he continued, "That is where your faith faded. I say it faded, because you had enough faith to ask him to help you in the first place. And he *did* help you, but it wasn't what you wanted. What was it that you said earlier—*I am a control freak!*" Josh was now smiling at me. He knew *I* knew he was right. He had just used my own words to give me my answer. *Clever! Real clever!* I smiled back at him.

His eyes were now fixed on me with his full attention. He had this way of asking me just the right way so that I knew the answer before he told me. And using my own words to show me was quite wise indeed.

"Donald, faith is powerful. Faith is the *knowing*, believing in the unknown. It is like the old saying: 'When a door shuts, another one will open.' You have heard this over and over again throughout your life, right?" It reminds me of the verse 'Knock and the door shall be opened.'"

He was looking at me for a response. I nodded, letting him know I understood. He then continued, "I want to take this a step further to emphasize faith. Most people, when they get to the point where the door must shut so another one will open, they want to keep their foot in the door that's shutting while trying to wait for the other door to open. It never works that way. It never will. You see, you must first be willing to let the door close *completely* before God will open the next door. Why would he do that, you ask? Faith! That's why. When both doors are shut, you are in complete darkness. That is where your faith in God comes in. You must trust in him to bring you out of the darkness by opening the other door for you. Once again, you must *let go and let God!*"

He looked over at me and winked. He smiled, motioning me to keep moving toward the gardens at the top of the hill.

He continued as we walked.

"God will never leave you, Donald. He cannot. He is a part of you and you are a part of him. You have a purpose for this life that God wants you to fulfill. Every one of his children has a purpose as well. All his children are different from each other, but God wants them all to fulfill their purpose nonetheless. Believing in him is showing him your faith. Jesus said, 'If you have the faith of a mustard seed, you can make the mountain move.'

"Do you know why I described faith as a mustard seed? It is because the seed is so small. If you have ever seen a mustard bush, though, it grows to be very large—to one of the largest in the area, if not the largest."

Josh paused a moment and then continued. "Faith illuminates hope. They go together. Hope gives purpose to what you are hoping for. Hope is the relevance of faith. When you reach out to God with your desires, you are placing faith in him to bring your desires into fruition. When one has both faith and hope, along with desire, they start developing into energy with actions of thought. The stronger your desire, faith, and hope are, the better chance you have to manifest your thoughts. *Faith* is believing you will receive God's favor. *Hope* is the passion of the soul to nourish what one cannot see in the moment. In Hebrews 6:19, it says, 'Hope is the anchor of the soul, firm and secure.' The end result is receiving the fruit of your desire. The scriptures say, 'The spirit of our faith is in our words.'"

We made our way up to the garden at the top of the hill. The flowers were in full bloom. He stopped talking as he approached a row of rosebushes with beautiful roses of several different colors. His eyes glistened as we got down on one knee and smelled their fresh aroma. It was a magnificent garden. The funny thing is, it had been here all along and I had never even been here to enjoy it. Josh motioned me to smell them. The air was filled with sweet smells of God's wonder. All these years I had missed them.

Then, without warning, he began to speak again. "The last thing I just said a few minutes ago stands to be absolute truth. Our words will always show the spirit of our faith." Josh waved his hands over everything around us. "Take a look around you. We need to praise God for all of this! We need to be grateful for all the blessings he has already given to us. We put our faith in him to show us the way. We stand firm in hope when we thank him for his present blessings and the ones yet to come. He wants you to receive your blessings. He loves you. You are his children. His faith in you is immeasurable. Praise him out loud. His blessings transpire for those who place him first in their hearts. There is abundant life right here before your eyes that God has given unto each of his children. They fail to see it by being blinded by their ambition. Just look around you when you are out among the crowds. You will now see it everywhere because I have now opened your eyes to it."

He reached out a hand to lift me off my knee. I stood up next to him. His words were straight and simple. His conviction was so very strong. I wanted what he had. He smiled, looking into my eyes, into my soul with his. I felt a peace I had never felt before and knew that everything was going to be okay. I looked down at my watch and realized I had to get back to work. We headed back to the car and stood there together a moment. I felt as if I had known Josh all my life. I felt so connected to him. He hadn't tried to push his beliefs on me; he had just answered my questions.

"Today I am here because you have always talked to me in faith throughout the years," he said, smiling radiantly. "God is always present, always! I wanted to come and shed some light on your heart. Your heart is true to your spirit; have the courage to follow it. It will lead you back home to me and my father, God Almighty."

I turned to look at him, but the sun was directly behind him and I had to squint to see him. He placed his hands on my shoulders. He continued speaking, his voice now a little stronger.

"Donald, always be grateful. Love God with all your heart. Praise him even in the bad times, showing him you have faith that it shall pass. Stay firm in your beliefs and convictions—with *hope*. You will know who is telling you the truth with your heart and spirit. You will know who to follow and which church to attend. I said many times you can tell by the fruits that they bear. Remember?"

I reached up and hugged him. I felt so complete at that moment. He held me, placing his hand on the back of my head. He then pulled me away so he could look right at me. He placed his hands on my face and wiped the tears flowing down my cheek. Then he pulled my head toward him and he kissed my forehead. I was speechless. He stood there not saying a word and then broke the silence with the most wonderful words I could have ever heard him say.

He said, "Donald, I love you!"

That very second I felt like the wealthiest man on earth. I stared into his eyes that had mesmerized me all day. They were now a soft blue. I reached out and touched his face with my right hand. He smiled and then turned toward the car. In my whole life I had never felt this way about a man—other than my father. He was so right. My eyes were now open. I was no longer blinded.

As we sat down in the car, he pulled a coin out of his pocket. It was a very old coin that had been worn down. He handed it to me.

"I want you to have this coin. I used a similar, old coin many years ago to share the word my father wanted me to share. The coin was a very old, rare coin. It had the face of Zeus on the front side and an eagle on the back. It was a coin from Egypt when Rome was there. I want you to have it to remind you of our time today. Listen, God is real. His son is real. His word is real all over this world. We both love you very much."

He then folded my hand over the coin. He looked back out at the park and then over to me.

"I told you today was going to be a great day," he said, his grin turning into a big smile. "We should say a prayer before we leave."

"Oh yes, a prayer would be nice right at this moment," I replied, still holding this rare old coin in my hand. Tears were filling up in my eyes.

We both bowed our heads. He began praying the most beautiful prayer I had ever heard. As he spoke, his voice seemed to float in the air. I felt the rays of sun beating on my face. It could not get any better than this. His prayer continued as my mind and heart were filled with his words of praise to our father. His voice was getting more and more faint at the end. I heard him say, "I bless Donald in your name, Father, and in mine, Christ Jesus, your son. Amen. *Donald, we love you.*"

Wait a minute. He was saying that he is . . . I opened my eyes. *What happened? Where was I? This cannot be.* He was gone. In fact, I was sitting in my office. *Where was the park? The car? No, this could not have been a dream!* My heart was pounding now, almost out of my chest. I felt so desperate. I know this really happened. I looked at my watch. I couldn't believe it. It was just past nine o'clock. *It couldn't be. No! This could not have been a dream.* I just sat there in disbelief, bewildered. I started crying angrily, praying out loud like so many other times I had. "You cannot do this to me, Lord. This is not fair!"

A gust of wind surged through my office at that very moment. It blew right through me. It disappeared quickly. When it passed, I felt an overwhelming sense of peace and calm come over me.

My office door was closed. I sat and leaned back into my chair. I started going over in my head what had happened in this dream or vision. I didn't know what it was, but I knew it meant something. Then I remembered Josh coming into my office. He said we had talked to each other in the past. *Wait a minute—Jesus had always been my imaginary friend when I was a child.* I remembered the pond in the park and him saying the blessing, ending it by saying, "I bless this food in your name, Father, Amen." He had never said *in Jesus Christ's name.* He also knew the old man's name in the park. He called him *Gerald.* He told me he knew for a fact that Jesus was real. Then, oh yeah, when he mentioned the mustard seed story, he had said, "Do you know why I described faith with the mustard seed?" Then he said that my heart was true and that it would lead me back to him and his father. *Wow. This was so deep. It was him all along! Josh . . . Joshua was . . . was . . . Jesus!*

The next few minutes I started to write down as much as I could remember of this dream. I was still shocked it was not real. All my life I had wanted to meet him, and when I finally did, I did not know it was *him. Oh my gosh!* I remembered just about everything he had said to me in this dream or vision—or whatever it was. I wanted more—more time with him. I wanted more information. I wanted more insights. It was all so confusing, yet so wonderful at the same time. I smiled and closed my eyes, trying to remember his face.

Then a knock came from my office door that made me almost have a heart attack.

Startled, I jumped up and said, "Come in!"

In stepped Glorina. "Are you all right?" she asked, looking confused as she entered the room. I smiled and replied, "I couldn't be better. What a beautiful morning, isn't it?"

She acknowledged back that it was a beautiful day. She then handed me the resumés of the interviewees who were waiting for me outside. *Déjà vu!* I laughed to myself. I told her to start sending them in. I was ready for them. I had taken on Josh's smile. I was ready for the day. *Oh yes!* I thought to myself, *this is going to be a day to remember.*

VI

The whole morning was more or less about me remembering what took place in my dream or vision. When I interviewed each person that day, I really took an interest in their wants and needs. I finished with the last interviewee and told Glorina I was going out for lunch. I grabbed my car keys and headed for the car. I looked around thinking maybe by chance Josh—no, *Jesus*—would appear to me. He didn't. I started the car. The sun was very bright, so I reached over for my sunglasses. *What was this?* Something caught my eye. *No way, it couldn't be!* It was the coin he had given me. *It was the rare coin! It wasn't a dream! It was all real!* I clenched my hand into a tight fist. Tears of joy flowed from my eyes. *He was here.* Then I remembered the last thing he had said to me: "Donald, we love you!"

I headed for the park to enjoy lunch outside and to smell the roses, knowing my life had just changed forever.

The End

Photo of the front of the coin

Photo of the back of the coin

Lightning Source UK Ltd.
Milton Keynes UK
UKOW06f1811140715

255190UK00004B/234/P